The Divorce

& Other Poems

Andrew Aldred

chipmunkapublishing
the mental health publisher

Andrew Aldred

Published by
Chipmunkapublishing
United Kingdom

http://www.chipmunkapublishing.com

Copyright © 2016 Andrew Aldred

ISBN   978-1-78382-256-0

About The Author

Andrew Aldred is an ex-soldier and Falklands veteran. He became ill in the army and suffered a twenty year psychotic illness resulting in ten years in hospital. He suffers from depression, paranoia and a bipolar condition. His illness is treatable and he has come out of hospital some years ago and come off his Home Office section. He has held various jobs and currently works at Prestwich Hospital assisting in running Creative Writing and ICT courses. He has recently split up with his wife and partner of the last eight years and is currently getting divorced.

Eurovision

He cuts a lonely and pathetic figure
Stood all alone in the centre of the stage
A man in drag with a beard
We are all watching him on television
And we are confused about his gender
But come to collecting the votes in
And this act is doing extremely well
I know the song was good
Something Shirley Bassey would have sang in the
seventies
As they count the votes
They make jokes about shaving the beard off
And I would have preferred it
If he had gone on as a gay man
Or a pretty woman
And as he wins the competition
I realise I am out of tune with Eurovision
And the rest of the world

Claw Back the Deficit

The government has decided
That we should no longer be in debt
That means that David Cameron
Is going to take money off you and me
To pay off the National debt
Personal Independence Payment is coming in
To replace Disability Living Allowance
And save three billion pounds
That means that we will all get less
And the government will retain more of its money
To pay off out debt
Until the country has started making money
On a large scale
And we can have it back
If they see fit
But the world is becoming more competitive
And there is less money to go round
If they want to export to the rest of the world
They will have to finance it
Off the backs of the poor

Plastic Surgery

I saw a bunch of Doctors
Doing something abnormally worthwhile
For a group of people working in the "beauty"
trade
A group of plastic surgeons no less
Who worked all year round on the rich and famous
And then took a holiday
To work on badly disfigured and diseased children
In Africa and Asia
It was on my television
And it brought it home to me
What plastic surgery should be about
Not vanity but acceptability
To create something normal instead of an
aberration
Of bigger lips and breasts and penises
Something that could actually make life better for
someone
Instead of just boosting an ego large enough
To cut off someone's nose in order to spite their
own face

Growing Older

We're all a bit more portly
As time goes on
Prescription drugs and alcohol
Have got us putting weight on
I'm beginning to feel my age
And a little more than that
Lack of exercise and arthritis
And a need to have a nap
My new job has got me worried
Will I be able to keep up?
Will my duties as a husband
Be all that I can do?
Take care of her daughter and her mother
And look after her too
I'm getting towards fifty
And desperately need to relax
But life won't wait for me
And I need to have a nap

Money

The world has been divided in conflict recently
Syria, Egypt, Afghanistan, the Congo
And countless other places
It all costs money
And keeps costing money
We are shopping in charity shops these days
Living off other people's cast offs
When I hear there's a disaster in the Philippines
I know where my money is going
India is sending a rocket to Mars
It will probably be very good for their industry
As the technology has a knock-on effect
It will cost a fraction as much
As our new railway from London to Birmingham
Bill Gates has rid a continent of disease
Through his contribution to world aid
Everyone's going crazy spending money
To keep the world spinning around
I just hope we keep in orbit

Fallen Hero

He served in Ireland and Iraq
And for two years in the Afghanistan war zone
But this marine has to face a long time in prison
For killing a wounded insurgent
I wonder whether he's happy with who he is
Whether he sleeps at night?
Or just keeps going through the nightmares?
What life is there left for him?
Just more death and violence
Another War Hero behind the gates of a prison
And maybe I agree that is the best place for him
But this man needs help
If he's ever going to see any sort of normality
In his life again
A man who has suffered so much needs sympathy
But all he will get is a kick in the teeth
Another wake-up call on a cold morning
I wish he had not killed his enemy

The War to end all Wars

This was what they billed it as
After the Second World War had ended
The War to end all Wars
There will never be another
But there is, time after time
And country after country
There's always another dictator
To be put in his place
Another Civil War
To tear a country apart
Do we ever learn any lessons?
In all this greed, enmity and adversity
I don't think we do
We just carry on making the same mistakes
Everyone wants a long and happy life
Why do we spend so much time?
Digging our own graves?

Pop Stars

Have I been sat in this armchair long enough?
For Kylie Minogue and Robbie Williams
And all the rest of them
To grow old?
It's a staggering thought
They aren't meant to grow old
You sort of think they'll be young forever
And it's only the likes of me that gets arthritis
And has to have growths removed from their
mouth
Christina has put on weight
And so has Britney
Mariah's had surgery
And God knows what's happened to Madonna
Even Beyoncé is growing older in the face
Not even having millions of dollars
Can stop the age process
Even the stars will see their dotage
It's very uncomfortable for me to think about
I wonder what it's like for them.

Mining the Moon

I watched the latest "Despicable Me" cartoon
On the television this winter
And I thought of the Chinese government
Whilst the cartoon character stole the moon
Have we gone too far?
Or not far enough?
Is it not enough to rape our own planet?
Do we have to start on the surroundings?
Do we need the minerals and the money so
much?
We have to go to the moon and get them?
Will it start turning out of orbit?
Will that affect planet earth?
Is this not happening already?
Can we all not do with a bit less
In order to leave something behind
For our children?
The world is full of people
Who can't see the wood for the trees
And most of them are running the place

Worried and run off my feet

I'm worried about my own health
And that of my wife
We should give up drinking and smoking
And start a new life
I'm worried about our daughter
And our niece
Hoping they will last the course
And manage to grow older
Whilst still remaining in one piece
I've got an educational course to design
For my own place of work
Bathroom carpets to lay
Living rooms to paint
And a million other things to do
Most of all I've got to maintain
Some sort of faith
That it will all get done
And that I can escape
For a day or two sometimes
Without doing very much
To give myself a brief rest
In this endless race

Flashpoint

Everyone is trying to avoid World War three
Or mostly they are
Russia has come into play heavily again
After lying dormant for many years
In a new age of "perestroika"
They have a hard line president in Vladimir Putin
Made of the same stuff as Stalin
And all the rest of the Great Russian dictators
They wouldn't let the rest of the world
Sort Syria out
Instead leaving a huge bloodbath
Of civil war and unrest
Because they wanted to keep
Their puppet president in charge
And now there is trouble in Crimea
They have marched right in there
To supposedly save the nation
Who mostly speak Russian
But when will they back down?
Or indeed will they?
There are other dictators in the world
There's some idiot half my age
Supposedly running North Korea
And not doing a very good job
There's only one world
We don't want to blow it up

Abducted by Aliens

An aeroplane disappeared off the radar
Exactly a week ago
No one knows where it has gone
Or that's what they are telling us
Every day they give us a few more clues
As to where it has gone
But everyone knows
There's something going on
They switched the radar and the communications
system off
There's no sign of a crash landing
Two hundred and fifty people
Disappearing in the space of a few hours
Relatives going spare
At the airport officials
Pilots under investigation
As well as anyone else
Who was anything to do
With this unfortunate flight
They can say whatever they like
About this disappearance
But it is obvious to me
There's more going on than meets the eye
I wish they would all come clean
They're not telling me
That this flight has been abducted by aliens

The Floods

There's been floods in America
And a Tsunami in the Philippines
As well as a huge natural disaster
In Japan involving a nuclear power station
What is going wrong with the weather?
Is global warming catching up on us?
Will the natural balance of the world adapt?
Or will we all be underwater?
Do we need to cut our carbon emissions?
Switch to renewable energy?
Is the day of Noah's Ark coming?
Will we ruin the planet?
Before we find solutions to our own problems
That are eco-friendly?
I don't know
But I do know that previous to us
Other species have been prevalent
On mother earth
And they had their day
There are no longer any dinosaurs
Maybe all that will be left of us one day
Are fossils and bits of debris
Buried in rock

Worst Case Scenario

They took me off lithium
Earlier in the year
It was the tablet they prescribed
For manic depression
My kidneys were packing in
And needed a rest
Now it is ten months later
And my imagination is running riot
In the middle of the night
Everyone is dying
And so am I
My wife is leaving me
All the worst things are happening
But they are not
And it's so hard to reconcile
It's all in my head
I wish I could cast it all out
But I am thinking about going back on the tablets

The Sons of Want will not be Blest

We've got Alex Salmond in Scotland
Saying he wants Scottish Independence
Talking about Rob Roy
And Bonnie Prince Charlie
And then we've got Nick Farage in England
Talking a load of imperialist nonsense
About cricket and pubs
And being English
Opting out of Europe
And these people are actually getting taken
seriously
Because John Smith cannot afford his groceries
And he thinks he can fined
An easy way out
But there is no way out
Of recession and world poverty
What do we expect?
Where is the profit?
Where is the trade?
That is where the wealth is made
And there isn't enough there
For us and a lot of other countries
They would like to keep us together in Europe
But we are falling apart
Opting out of something greater
There is no unity
Only people fighting over small change
Doesn't anyone realise
We're all in this together?

Two Strikes and You're Out

I've heard about them in the news
Prisoners going on the run
They're on parole
Doing their last days inside
But the system gives them no hope
There's no next time for them
They've had enough
Justice has become too ruthless
They're going to get locked away forever
And they would rather it would be sooner
When are they going to realise
That crime doesn't pay
The buck has stopped
With the Ministry of Justice
No one feels any sympathy for them
They're going on the radio
Saying lock them in a box with nothing
And leave them to rot
I've been there myself
And I really hope I've learnt my lesson
But some people just don't
They think they're owed a living
As criminals and thugs
They won't all be coming home from prison one
fine day
They'll just die there

Mugged

I am staggering back from a pub
Somewhere in Aldershot
My friend has left me
To go it alone
Someone grabs me from behind
And puts me in a sleeper
On a deserted road
I'm unconscious
For God knows how long
I wake up
In the January snow
Wearing just a T shirt
I check out my wallet
All my money's gone
But at least they haven't taken my I.D.
I know I've been rolled
But it could have been so much worse
I pick myself up
And finish the walk home
Another sad night out

Girl with a Pram

I came into the flats one night
And saw a girl with a pram
She said she'd just had her baby
And only had another night with him
Before Social Services took him away
She said she wanted to go out tonight
She was a street girl from around the corner
And I lived in the flats for the mentally ill
On the main street
And she wanted me to look after the baby
I said of the child
"He looks so tough"
And told her I couldn't
As my flat was no place to look after a child
I went inside to drink a bottle of whisky
And wondered why the girl had brought him to me
Was there no one else?

Heart Attack

We've gone to bed
And sleep until four o clock in the morning
When my wife wakes up
And starts being sick over the side of the bed
I clean the mess up
And we phone for the duty doctor
But she gets more uncomfortable
As time goes on
She can't rest
And there's pain in her chest
And her arms
I phone for an ambulance
And try to keep her calm
Until they come
Try to get her to relax
And stay still
I open the front door
And pull on some clothes
And the ambulance arrives
They give her valium and morphine
And take us both to a hospital twenty miles away
Where she can be treated
For a blood clot on the heart
They give her the operation
An hour and a half never lasted so long
She's alive and her pain is eased
I breathe a sigh of relief
And give thanks to God

Turn it Off

I'm so fed up with the news these days
It is just so depressing
The next paedophile getting caught
All the people who were on telly
When you were a kid
Getting locked up in jail
And then there's the jihad
And the Islamic State
Who want to behead Western journalists
And the potential War with Russia
The world just seems to be falling down
Like a line of dominoes
I wish I could turn all these people off
Like the television
Get rid of them
And get on with something useful
I wish I could bear to watch
What's going on in the world today
But it's turning me right off
And I don't want to watch it on television

Forty a Day and Counting

We've cut down to twenty cigarettes a day
recently
It's a lot less than forty or sixty
We've invested in some E Cigarettes
To soften the blow
And hold off the cancer
To spend a bit less money
On this horrible and ridiculous habit
That permeates our life
It had got so bad
I was running out of shops to go to
And getting embarrassed
When other people were asking for ten
And I asked for eighty for my wife and myself
I don't want to be counting down to a fatal illness
I want to be counting some more money
I want to be counting less cigarettes smoked every
day
And a longer life expectancy

The War on Drugs

I watched a programme last night
About the war on drugs
Hosted by Russell Brand
Katy Perry's ex – no less
He cared a lot about the addicts
But came across as a frustrated junkie himself
And I'm not very sure his abstinence therapy
Was any sort of a cure for his addiction
But there's something of Russell Brand in me
My wife's just had a heart attack
Because of smoking cigarettes
We've both given up
But walking through town
I can smell everyone smoking
And I must admit it smells great
But what about the huge black market trade in drugs?
Would the trade not be better off
If it was run by governments
And regulated from top to bottom
From growing the stuff in plantations
To the selling and distribution of it
The governments would get the taxes
And people could have a safe fix
Like the "smoking kills" message on my last packet
Education and freedom of choice
Might be a better way of fighting
The war on drugs

Virtual Reality

Everyone's going mad on Facebook these days
I'm just going mad
With all the useless messages
It throws at me
The pretty blond girls
That keep appearing
The people I've never met
Wanting to be friends
Why did I join this stupid bit of software
That gives me so very little I want?
And lots of things I don't
Is this the future?
Am I expected to spend time on this?
I have got a real life
With a real family
And some real friends
And no time for trawling around websites
Looking for trouble
Or telling people exactly what I'm up to
When it's none of their business
I've got a telephone
I can write letters
I can spend time with people
And I don't need virtual reality to do that

Casualty of Sex

I used to know a few girls
Who were in the trade
I used to meet them
In the local mental hospital
When I went there for a rest
Every time the bastards drove me insane
I never knew what was going on
I never tried to find out
I felt the paranoia
Every night as I went to sleep
Never had a sex life through my twenties and
thirties
Just a psychotic illness
Committing a crime was my way out
My body couldn't take it any more
And neither could my brain
I got a home office section
And judged insane
Because some set of maggots
Couldn't leave me alone
I had a house
But it was never a home
I lost everything
And somehow got it back
Youth and a figure
Are now things that I lack

The Great Divide

They've got boats full of Syrians
Coming to Europe
African refugees
We don't really want to let them in
They're people with real issues to deal with
We've just sit around worrying
About gluten allergies
About obesity
And giving up smoking
Life's already hard enough
Because of the age of austerity
We've got clean water
More than enough food
Accommodation to live in
We've lost touch with reality
We all want the latest x-box
And a new laptop
A brand new mobile phone and a car
We all think we're due these things
In our spoilt Western society
What are we really doing for the rest of the world?
We send our soldiers over
Give them aid with our charities to ease our
collective conscience
But we shouldn't wonder when they think our way
of life is wrong
One half of the world has more than enough
And the other wants to blow it up

Television Fugitive

There was a film called Joyride on this afternoon
A young man had his head crushed by a truck
axle
Very graphically
Broadchurch is on this evening
A series all about paedophiles and murder
Is this all we have for entertainment?
Or can we call it that?
Why is anybody interested?
Have we all not got enough going on in our sad
little lives
Without the television?
And my wife's daughter thinks it's wrong
Because the music channel is sexualising children
But I think it goes a great deal farther than that
There's incest on the soap channel
There's racism on the comedy channel
There's a load of filth on the adult channel
That you have to pay for
The rest of the crap you get for free
With sky television
I have to crawl into the conservatory
To get away from it all
Why did they get rid of the seventies?
Where did it all go wrong?
All I know is that I'm hiding from the television
And I don't want it in my life

More Morose than Usual

There's no doubt
I'm more morose than usual tonight
I've drank a lot of beer over Christmas
And it must be catching up with me
Or so my wife tells me
And I'd better listen to her
Or there's no telling what will happen
So I grit my teeth
And sort myself out
Which is twice as hard to do
Because we've given up smoking recently
But I can't stand her being upset
And the beer will always get the blame
So I'd better stop drinking
Lighten up and get sober again
And face the New Year with a smile

The Covert Revolution

The Labour Party have just been on television
again
Saying how they're going to save the NHS
Another empty promise
Because you know whatever party gets in
They're only going to dismantle it further
Make more privatisations
Build more hospitals we don't need
And waste money on things
Other than health care
It takes a week to see your GP these days
You used to be able to get an appointment the
following day
Accident and Emergency is full
It takes longer to get seen than it used to
Everything is much more inefficient
When it should be the other way around
It's all to cock
They've ruined the NHS
And that will be their excuse
To replace it with something else
That we all have to pay for

Breakfast TV

See them all talking around a table
With their shining white teeth
That would put crocodiles and sharks to shame
Promoting their latest stint on television
And now something has come on
That really makes me sick
Some do-gooder on a train
Giving a mum a fiver
For telling her young son how to behave
In front of the said gentleman
They are organising a reunion
And there he is with a silly silk scarf
And his spectacles balanced on his forehead
The mum's hair-do must have cost a hundred
pounds
What is it all about?
Telling us how to behave
And it's taking up time on a national television
programme
This is something I really don't need

Desensitised

We've each had a couple of cans tonight
We might as well have had
Two litres of vodka each
It's the same old shit on the telly
Little more than a joke
Bizarre soap operas
And then there's the programme
About the mega brothels in Germany
Some girl of twenty four years
Saying she's been with fifteen thousand men
And somehow she can be bothered to get out of
bed
To do it all again
But business is slack
So she's got to move on
And I wonder about us
Where did we lose the urge?
Is sex some sort of disease?
That too much of it is the only cure
I really wish we could be bothered any more
But there's things that are more important
Like looking after our grandson
My wife's mother and daughter
Having a holiday
We're in our late forties
And dead on our feet

Andrew Aldred

Motivation

We saw a house going for forty grand
We're thinking about buying it
And doing it up
Turning it over and making a profit
But why?
It would be something to do
But do we really have the energy
Is the gigantic headache it would create?
Really worth the extra ten grand
It would make on sale
Just another pipe dream
We've only just sorted out our own house
We don't need another one
Leave it to someone who does

Disability Hate Crime

They've been talking about genetic imperfection
Since some set of maniacs
Created Dolly the sheep
Now they're on about having three parents
Forgetting what they had outlawed
Twenty years ago
They forget that the imperfections in us
Are what makes us human
What makes us real people
They should be embracing disability
Instead of trying to eradicate it
With genetic engineering
It harks back to the Nazis
The idea of the super race
If you play God too much
You may have to answer to him
God was never a scientist or a doctor

Women in Religion

You can have a woman archbishop for me
Or even a woman Pope
Women should have a voice in religion
And a larger one than they do have
Particularly in Islam and the Catholic Church
Half the people in the world are women
They should be represented
Fairly and equally
Their views valued and noted
And their issues listened to
In religion and everywhere else

The Beauty Trade

I took my wife to a hairdresser today
Sometimes I take her to a beautician
It really baffles me
Why anyone bothers with all of this
False nails, eyelashes and hair
And then there's the serious stuff
The cosmetic surgery
I think my wife looks great
Without a head of false hair
What's the point in getting it stitched in
When it's not permanent anyway
You pay a hundred quid
For something you can't keep
That's maintenance for you
All these women keeping up with each other
And men as well
I hope it makes them feel good about themselves
Because it does nothing for me

The Hunting Ground

They're going out tonight
In their skimpy dresses
And high heeled shoes
Looking as good as they can
The boys are no different
Some of them wear make up
Well doused in aftershave
They're all going to the hunting ground
The town centre late at night
They're all looking for love
Or so they say
When all most of them want
Is to get laid for free
And get drunk and dance
We used to go out
And mingle with the pretty faces
Fight our way to the bar
It was something of a tradition
But we got married and moved on
Left it to the next generation
Swapped the nightclubs for television
And now I'm a bit older
I look back and wonder
Was it really as good
As we thought it was?

Spider

My wife went upstairs
To the bedroom and shouted me
Another emergency
I stopped what I was doing
And went upstairs
To witness her horror
Something the size of a tarantula
Crouched still on the wall
I crushed the beast
Under my hand
He looked a lot smaller
Wrapped up in a ball
I put him in the bin
Which I emptied outside
And collapsed with my wife
And the stress of it all

To You

I'll raise a glass to you anytime
For the last eight years
You've been my partner in crime
From the love we've made
To the money we've saved
We'll make it to our graves
This time
I waited for a year for you
Incarcerated in a hospital
My money I gave to you
Its fine
You've had two mental breakdowns
And a heart attack
But I've been there for you
We've got a grandson
And you're daughter back
We'll make it to the end
Of the line

A Lucky Win

For once in my life
I'm a gambling man
I believe in a horse
And I know that he can
I watch as they start
Gallop down the field
A horse loses his rider
My horse is midfield
As they progress
I can't believe my eyes
My horse has pulled level
And the favourite is tired
I never felt so lucky
As he crossed the line
And I can worry about debt
Some other time

Accelerating Towards Death

She's on a psychotic mission
Hurtling around in taxis
Drinking bars dry
Smoking sixty a day
After her heart attack
She'd rather be anywhere
Than at home with me
And what is it all for?
This performance
She's asserting her independence
With my money
She'll run out of steam
When I pull the plug on her
But by then it will be too late
For us and her
All I can do is call the Doctor
And the Social Worker
All day and night
She's accelerating towards death

Dreams

My dreams are always stark and real
Whether they are the darkest nightmare
Or mad fantasy
They have never been the same since childhood
I would always be in the crow's nest
On the mast of a ship
And I would go to sleep
And always fall off and wake up
I have dreamt I could fly
Had the deepest sexual fantasies
Had night terrors for years
But now I dream a lot less
And sleep a lot more
My mind is less troubled
As life goes on

Over Rated

Drinking must be the most over-rated pastime
On God's green earth
I see them at five o clock
Drunk and shouting
As I walk to my car through the town centre
What are they about?
A bunch of empty heads
And my wife would trade
A life at home with no worries
For this battleground
I don't understand
And that's why we're apart
She hasn't moved on with the times
She doesn't realise she's forty seven
And has had a heart attack recently
Is this all that's left for her?
I hate to say it
But that's what she wants
And I can't share it with her any more

Christmas Tree

Nobody had a lot of money in those days
We had just moved into a new house
And my parents were mortgaged up to the hilt
We couldn't afford a Christmas tree
So one day we got into my Dad's car
And went for a trip in the country
In the twilight hours
We found a plantation of trees
By the side of the road
My Dad switched the lights off
And we went for a short walk
We crossed a barbed wire fence
My brother and I took turns to saw the trunk
And when that was done
We took our spoils to the car
I'm sure we had a better Christmas
Because of the stolen tree

All My Love

She took all of my love
I looked after her for eight years
Through four breakdowns and a heart attack
But she wouldn't stop drinking and smoking
She would run out on the town by herself
Leaving me alone in the house
And when things went bad between us
She wouldn't admit I had a point of view
She wanted all the money and the house as well
I can't stand any more wrangling
I don't want to fight any more
You took me for granted
You took all my love
And now it's forever yours

www.ingramcontent.com/pod-product-compliance
Lightning Source LLC
Chambersburg PA
CBHW020246290326
41930CB00038B/529